Advice given to a young native American at initiation:

As you go the way of life,
You will see a great chasm.
Jump.
It is not as wide as you think!

Lucky Duck is more than a publishing house and training agency. George Robinson and Barbara Maines founded the company in the 1980s when they worked together as a head and psychologist developing innovative strategies to support challenging students.

They have an international reputation for their work on bullying, self-esteem, emotional literacy and many other subjects of interest to the world of education.

George and Barbara have set up a regular news-spot on the website. Twice yearly these items will be printed as a newsletter. If you would like to go on the mailing list to receive this then please contact us:

e-mail newsletter@luckyduck.co.uk   website www.luckyduck.co.uk

How to use the CD-ROM

The CD-ROM contains PDF files, labelled 'Worksheets.pdf' which contain worksheets for each lesson in this resource. You will need Acrobat Reader version 3 or higher to view and print these resources.

The documents are set up to print to A4 but you can enlarge them to A3 by increasing the output percentage at the point of printing using the page set-up settings for your printer.

To photocopy the worksheets directly from this book, align the edge of the page to be copied against the leading edge of the copier glass (usually indicated by an arrow).

ISBN: 1 904 315 37 2

Published by Lucky Duck Publishing Ltd.

www.luckyduck.co.uk

Commissioning Editor: George Robinson

Editor:ial Team Wendy Ogden, Mel Maines, Sarah Lynch

Production manager: Helen Weller

Illustrations: Adrian Osborne

© A. Fuller, R. Bellhouse, G. Johnston 2004

ed by Antony Rowe Limited

rinted in Australia by New Litho

s reserved. No part of this publication may be reproduced, stored in a retrieval transmitted in any form, or by any means, electronic, mechanical, photocopying, or otherwise, without the prior, written permission of the publisher.

y pages marked as handouts, certificates or overhead foils are extended to of the publication for his/her use.

Author to be identified as Author of this work has been asserted by him/ with the Copyright, Design and Patents Act, 1988.

Adolescents - Snappy Ideas

Contents

About Snappy Ideas 5
Session One: The History of Spitting 7
Session two: Communication and Distortion 11
Session three: The Ancient Art of Palmistry 14
Session four: Self-awareness – How People See Me 16
Session five: Substance and Style 18
Session six: Seven Wonders of the Ancient World 19
Session seven: Opinions and Prejudices 21
Session eight: Local Heroes 33
Session nine: The Fickle Finger of Fate 34
Session ten: Predictions 41
Session eleven: Future Predictors 44
Session twelve: Predictions about Me 47
Session thirteen: Fashion Parade 49
Session fourteen: Great First Lines of Books 51
Session fifteen: The Day I Discovered My Bottom 55
Session sixteen: What's Cool? 58
Session seventeen: Nothin', Dunno and Whatever! 60
Session eighteen: Popular Culture 62
Session nineteen: The Winners! 64
Session twenty: Dating Agency 67
Session twenty-one: Careers – what am I good at? 74
Session twenty-two: What's My Career? 83

Bibliography 85

Inyahead Vision Statement

We aim to provide educationally based training and programmes that promote well-being and resilience and are characterised by creativity, excitement, integrity, fun and collaborative working relationships.

Underlying Principles

The following principles guide and inform all of our work:

1. A shared vision and commitment to people.
2. Sensitivity to the stages of development in people's lives.
3. A commitment to supportive relationships.

About Snappy Ideas

Three of the great changes in human life occur during the adolescent years:
- The ability to think abstractly
- The commencement of reproductive capacity
- The beginnings of self definition, identity and independence.

In Snappy Ideas we attempt to provide a set of activities to help young people explore some of the important questions that confront them during adolescence. The activities may be used flexibly and adapted for different purposes depending on the specific key learning area or objective of the teacher using the activity.

The main themes of the resource are:
- Identity
- Resilience
- Success
- Relationships
- Conformity
- Future
- Careers

The activities have been extensively trialled in Australian schools by teachers with varied levels of experience and confidence, as well as with students from diverse backgrounds.

Cautionary note: Teachers might need to protect young people who are divulging information that is harmful to themselves or others. Knowing how to sensitively interrupt is a skill that teachers should feel aware of and comfortable with. When teachers are unsure or concerned, they should seek further advice from a trained professional. If a teacher has concerns, or is unsure about the appropriateness of any activity, they should seek further advice, or refrain from using it.

Circle Time – promoting friendly behaviour in circles

Learning about empathy is best when friendly behaviour is evident. While teachers have many different strategies for developing friendly behaviour, we believe sitting students in circles encourages trust, co-operation and shared consideration.

What is Circle Time?

Circle Time is a structured, regular occasion when a class group meets in a circle to speak, listen, interact and share concerns. Circle Time is simple and routine. It provides a forum for students in which they feel comfortable to share and express their thoughts and feelings.

Why use a circle?

The circle is a symbol of unity and co-operation. It indicates that the group is working together to support one another and take equal responsibility for addressing issues and solving problems.

What is the role of the teacher?

Teachers facilitate. They provide a supporting and accepting environment and take part in all activities.

What is the process of Circle Time?

The three key elements of traditional Circle Time are:

- Understanding and valuing myself
- Understanding and valuing others
- Having positive relationships with others.

How is Circle Time organised?

It is best to allow pupils (whatever age) to sit on chairs which are placed in a circle with the teacher as part of it. However, if it is necessary for children to sit on the floor each child should have a carpet square. This is not just for comfort. It helps to maintain the circle formation. Everyone needs to be able to see everyone else and be able to establish eye contact.

Circle Time needs to be a planned and regular occurence – at least once a week.

Circle Time rules

Three rules for Circle Time are:

Listening to others

Giving one person the right to speaking without being interrupted and everyone having a turn to speak.

Speaking in a friendly way

Giving compliments, asking and respecting others' rights to their own thoughts and feelings. Avoiding teasing, negative comments and put downs.

The right to pass

Giving everyone the right not to speak.

Session One: The History of Spitting

Purpose

To build trust and encourage participation.

Process

Arrange seats in a circle.

Ask the students to sit in the circle.

Explain that there are three rules that are important when sitting in the circle:

1. If you do not wish to say anything, you have a right to pass.
2. You should be respectful of others by listening when they are speaking.
3. You should be positive to others and avoid making negative comments, teasing and laughing inappropriately.

Ask students to proceed around the circle and say their name, as well as the name of the person on either side of them.

Discuss

How does sitting in a circle feel different from sitting behind a desk?

Play a mixing game. Ask students to change seats if they:

- Like hip hop
- Like soaps
- Like school
- Like playing sport
- Think school uniforms are necessary
- Usually complete their homework

NB Or other statements relevant to the group.

Hand out, *The European History of Spitting*. Ask students to read and complete the questions.

Discuss questions.

Go around the circle and ask students to complete the sentence:

"A manner that is important to me is…"

Discussion questions

Why do we have manners?

How have manners for spitting changed over the years?

How do manners differ between cultures, such as hugging, kissing, shaking hands and queuing?

Additional Activity

Research another form of manners: burping, toilet cleaning, teeth cleaning, opening doors, walking alongside someone, groping - you know the kind of thing!

The History of Spitting

Good manners are good manners. Right?

Wrong!

Manners have changed dramatically over the centuries. Let's consider the history of spitting.

The European History of Spitting

1. Do not spit over or on the table (English, 1463)
2. Turn away when spitting, lest your saliva fall on someone. If anything purulent falls to the ground it should be trodden on (Erasmus, 1530)
3. You should abstain from spitting at the table, if possible (Italian, 1558)
4. Formerly it was permitted to spit on the ground before people of rank... today, that is an indecency (French, 1572)
5. Frequent spitting is disagreeable. At important houses, one spits into one's handkerchief.
6. Do not spit so far that you have to look for the saliva to stamp on it (Liege, 1714)
7. It is very ill-mannered to swallow what should be spat... After spitting into your handkerchief, you should fold it once, without looking at it, and put it in your pocket (La Salle, 1729)
8. It is unpardonably gross for children to spit in the faces of their playmates (La Salle, 1774)
9. Spitting is at all times a disgusting habit. Besides being coarse and atrocious, it is very bad for the health (English, 1859).
10. 'No Spitting' notices were not displayed on London buses until the 1960s.*

Spitting wasn't challenged until the 1700s and through the next two centuries expectations about when and where one could spit became more restrictive until in the twentieth century when a total ban on spitting became effective.

*Information from: Davies N, (1997), Europe: A History, Pimlico Press, London

Worksheet: The History of spitting

What might happen if people spit at the table?
....
....
....
....

Explain whether there are times when spitting is acceptable?
....
....
....
....

Describe three manners that are important to you.
....
....
....
....
....

Session two: Communication and Distortion

Purpose ruler

To assist students to become aware of their communication patterns and how messages can be distorted or misunderstood.

Process

1. Provide a ruler, pencil and one blindfold for every group of five students.
2. Photocopy Distortion worksheet and cut into cards.
3. Explain you are about to do an experiment about how clearly we communicate.
4. Divide students into teams of five.
5. Seat them in lines.
6. Give the first student a card with a picture, for example, bread, light bulb, sun, person under pressure, vet with dog, computer, armchair or wind generators. That person then describes the picture to another but cannot use its name. That person then describes to the next and the next. The last person should draw it.
7. The person with the original card shows it to the class.
8. The last in the line then shows their drawing to the class.
9. The class votes on how similar they are, giving a rating from 1 to 10.

Discussion questions

How do things people say get distorted?

When are stories about people most likely to get distorted?

How does it feel when stories about you are distorted?

Worksheet: Distortion activity

Worksheet: Distortion activity

ADOLESCENTS: SNAPPY IDEAS

Session three: The Ancient Art of Palmistry

Purpose
To encourage students to consider how much they might influence their future.

To explore whether identity is a choice or pre-determined.

Process
1. Ask students to sit in a circle.
2. Around the circle, number the students in order. All of the odd numbers turn to their left to form a pair with the even numbered person next to them.
3. Partners interview each other and write down three of their partner's most favourite things.
4. Play a game where the members of the circle try to guess each student's favourite things. The player being questioned answers 'yes' or 'no', and might give hints. For example, if the favourite thing was basketball, the hints might include, a sport…, a sport played in teams…, a sport using a round ball…etc.
5. Distribute Who am I? worksheet. Ask students to read the sheet and complete the questions. (NB: Students might either discuss their palms, or write down their findings.)
6. Ask students to complete the statement:

    "One thing I enjoy most is…"
7. Discuss questions.

Discussion questions
'Character is destiny' (George Elliot)

Discuss:

What the statement means.

Whether you agree with it.

Are people born the way they are, or do they choose who they will become?

Worksheet: Who am I?

The art of palmistry or hand-reading has been around a long time. The idea is that someone's character, personality and even their future can be told by reading the lines on their hand. Do you believe it?

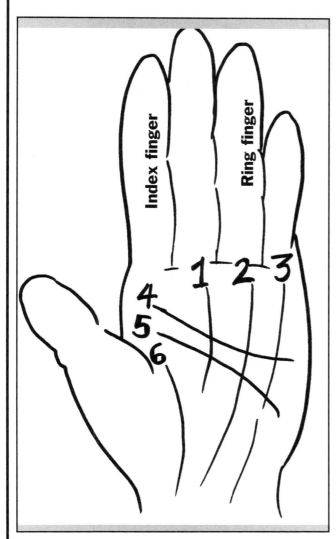

Let's see.

If your index finger is longer than your ring finger you are supposed to like money more than art. If your ring finger is longer than your index finger you are meant to prefer art to money.

The Line of Fate is line 1 - the clarity of this line is supposed to tell you how much of your line is determined by factors other than your own decisions.

The Line of Health is line 2 and is usually quite short. The clearer, the healthier.

The Line of Scientific Gifts is line 3. How distinct is yours?

The Line of the Heart is line 4 - some people say by having an unbroken line means deep love and faithfulness.

The Line of Will is line 5 and is supposed to tell you how strong is your will power. A comparison of lines 5 and 1 is supposed to tell you how much of what happens in your life will be determined by chance or fate and how much will be as a result of your own will power.

The Line of Life is line 6 and its distinctness and sharpness is supposed to be a sign of good health.

Instructions

1. Read your own palm.
2. Now read the palm of the person sitting next to you.

Session four: Self-awareness – How people see me

Purpose

To examine self-awareness.

Process

1. Hand out a survey to each student.
2. Arrange the students into groups of three.
3. Ask for a volunteer from each group.
4. Each group member completes the survey about the volunteer. (For example, three surveys will be completed for each volunteer.) Ask students to complete the surveys without referring to the answers of other students. The volunteers complete the survey about themselves.
5. In groups of three, compare survey results.
6. Discuss:
   - How were the answers similar or different?
   - What other characteristics does the volunteer have that are not in the table?

Discussion questions

Do we really know what we are like?

Are we always learning new things about ourselves?

Do people change with time and experience, or are they always basically the same?

Worksheet: Self-awareness – How People See Me

Complete the following survey with 10 equalling 'people are very likely to see me this way' and 0 being 'people are very unlikely to see me this way'.

Characteristic	Rating
Funny	. . . .
Honest	. . . .
Hard working	. . . .
Sporty	. . . .
Creative	. . . .
Angry	. . . .
Friendly	. . . .
Shy	. . . .
Loud	. . . .
Calm	. . . .

Session five: Substance and Style

Purpose

To explore self-image.

Process

1. Ask students to bring five images each that are cut out of magazines. Pair students asking each to bring images relating to different categories: food, home, animals, uncool, faces, sport, holidays, nature. Pin these images up around the room.
2. Ask students to look at the images. After a few minutes select one to three images that students feel relate to them. (Once a student takes an image it is unavailable to other students.)
3. Students design a poster that represents who they are.
4. Students share their posters with the rest of the class, and explain how it represents them.

Discussion questions

If you completed a poster in five years' time:

How might it have changed?

Session six: Seven Wonders of the Ancient World

Purpose

To consider what inspires students.

To consider similarities and differences.

Process

1. Explain to students:

In the ancient world there were seven wonders:
- The Colossus of Rhodes
- The Hanging Gardens of Babylon
- The Lighthouse of Alexandria
- The Great Pyramid of Giza
- The Temple of Artemic
- The Mausoleum at Halicanassum
- The Statue of Zeus at Olympia.

2. Discuss why these were wonders of the world?
3. Break into groups, and ask each group to choose seven wonders of the world today.
4. Ask groups to report back to the class, and explain their choices.
5. Ask students to complete the worksheet.
6. Report back to the class, noting the differences and similarities.

Optional – My Personal Oasis

Discuss:

1. What is a personal oasis?
   - A fertile place in the midst of a desert.
   - A place where you can re-fuel and replenish yourself.
2. Do any students have their own personal oasis?
3. How might a personal oasis be helpful?
4. Ask students to write a short description of their own personal oasis and what makes it special to them.

Discussion questions

What were the most common similarities among students?

What were the most common differences among students?

Worksheet: Seven Wonders of the World

List your own seven modern wonders of life:

Wonderful taste ....

Wonderful sight ....

Wonderful sound ....

Wonderful touch ....

Wonderful smell ....

Wonderful memory ....

Wonderful thing ....

Session seven: Opinions and Prejudices

Purpose
Exploring acceptance, tolerance and difference.

Process
1. Ask students to sit in a circle and change places if they agree:
   - The world would be a better place if everybody had the same opinions.
   - Everyone has a right to their own opinion.
   - Everybody is basically the same as everyone else.
   - Everybody is basically different from everyone else.
2. Ask students to turn to the person on their left and discover two similarities they have in common.
3. Proceed around the circle and ask each pair to explain:
   - their two similarities
   - how they feel about these.
4. Discuss as a group:
   - How does discovering things in common with other people make you feel?
5. Ask students to turn to the person on their left and discover two differences they have in common.
6. Proceed around the circle and ask each pair to explain:
   - their two differences
   - how they feel about these.

7. Discuss as a group:
   - How does having differences with other people make you feel?
8. Make up a set of cards and like and dislike signs for each end of the room.
9. Ask students to form a horse-shoe. Distribute cards of imaginery friends. Place a **like** sign at one end of the horse-shoe, and a **dislike** sign at the opposite end. Explain to students that you are going to read a series of statements. You want them to think about the statement in terms of how they would feel about their imaginary friend. If they believe the statement would cause them to like the friends on their card more, they move toward the like sign, and vice versa if the statement would cause them to dislike their friends more. If they are unsure or neutral, remain towards the middle of the continuum, about half way between the two signs.
10. After students have placed themselves along the continuum, ask them to explain their reasons for their placement.
11. Ask students to complete the worksheet.

Discussion questions

What is meant by the saying: 'Birds of a feather flock together'?
What motivates people to want to be the same as other people?
What is a 'bigoted' opinion?
Brainstorm examples of bigoted opinions.

Parent	Aunt
Uncle	Friend

Stranger	Brother
Sister	Teacher

Dance Instructor	Movie Star
Religious Leader	Sports Coach

| Musician | Partner |

| Work Colleague | Boss |

Doctor	Politician
Soldier	Hairdresser

Opinions and Prejudices

Statements

How would you feel if you discovered your imaginary person:

- was kind to animals
- believed in a different religion from you
- belonged to an unusual cult
- liked the same things as you
- showed off by making fun of other people
- was the same star sign as you
- took illegal drugs
- sympathised with a terrorist group
- supported a different football team to you
- believed in the death penalty for some crimes
- was incredibly rich
- had different skin colour to you
- was faithful to their partner
- had a different partner every time you saw them
- had been involved in a same-sex relationship
- hated people from a particular country
- was drunk at a nightclub and beat someone up?

Worksheet: Going Tribal

List all the groups to which you belong (friendship, gang, sport, hobby, club, family).

....

....

....

....

....

....

Worksheet: Opinions and Prejudices

Choose one group of which you particularly like being a member.

- Why are you a member of this group?
  ....
  ....
  ....

- Will you always be a member of this group?
  ....
  ....
  ....

- List one or two similarities you have with other members of this group.
  ....
  ....
  ....

- List one or two differences you have with other members of this group.
  ....
  ....
  ....

- Why does your group stay together?
  ....
  ....
  ....

Session eight: Local Heroes

Purpose
To examine the concept of resilience.

Preparation
Local Heroes is an activity where students become involved in studying resilience by developing a biography of a local person (or family member) who has been resilient in their lives.

Process
1. Divide the class into groups.
2. Ask them to nominate a Local Hero.
3. Ask the groups of students to discover:
   - What was hard in their hero's life? For example, difficulties growing up, working at their jobs, in their families etc.
   - What their hero did to survive the hard times?
   - How their hero got on with their life?
   - How their hero began enjoying themselves again?
4. Make a plan to collect the information.
5. Once students have collected their information, they might create a story board of their hero's life based on interviews, pictures and historical events.

Discussion questions
What are the most important things that help people survive hard times?

Session nine: The Fickle Finger of Fate

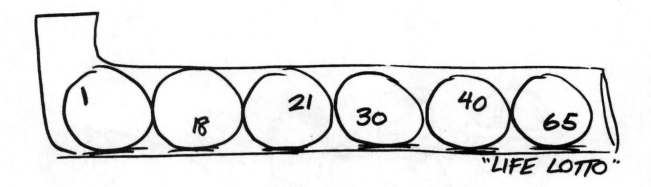

Purpose
To explore elements of a resilient life.

Preparation
One set of cards for every group of five students. Ideally these could be photocopied on different coloured paper to distinguish between the years. Cut and prepare into cards.

Process
1. Divide the class into teams of five.
2. Designate one member of each group as the dealer.
3. Explain that the 'Fickle Finger of Fate' is a game in which you have to imagine that your group is about to have a series of reunions, one year from today, ten years from today, twenty years from today, thirty years from today, forty years from today and fifty years from today.
4. At each reunion, the group (or member) will be given a task to be completed.
5. Distribute a set of cards arranged in year order (Year One, Year Ten, Year 20 through to Year 50) to each dealer. Ask the dealer to avoid mixing up the years.
6. Each player receives one card initially for year one.
7. When the initial task is complete, deal the cards for Year 10 and complete the task.
8. Repeat this process through to 50 years.
9. Ask players to keep their cards.
10. When the game is finished, ask each player to explain:
    - What has happened to them.
    - How they feel about their life.

Discussion questions
If you could change one thing, what would it be?

Lay out the cards in groups. Ask players to choose those cards that represent the best and the worst possible life.

Worksheet: Fickle Finger of Fate
One Year into the Future

Task: Determine how you inter-relate and answer the questions.

One Year Later
You are now the best friend of the person whose birthday is earliest in the year. (Why?)

One Year Later
You and the person who has most recently eaten a Mars bar take up an obscure hobby together.

(What could it be?)

One Year Later
You and the person whose birthday is latest in the year hang around with the person who most likes chocolate. (What sorts of things do you do together?)

One Year Later
You and the person with the longest hair in the group have a falling out.

(What is it over?)

One Year Later
You share an annoying habit with the youngest person in the group.

(Discuss what it is.)

ADOLESCENTS: SNAPPY IDEAS

Worksheet: Fickle Finger of Fate
Ten Years into the Future

Task: Work out how everyone interrelates and explain how close you are to other members of the group.

Ten Years Later
You are studying cartooning up north and are a close friend with another member of the group.

Ten Years Later
You are working as a lead singer in a band based on the west of the continent, and owe another member of the group a lot of money.

Ten Years Later
You have a partner and a family and visit the person living up north.

Ten Years Later
You are closest to the person in the west, but live down south.

Ten Years Later
You won't speak to the person in the west but complain about them to the person up north.

Worksheet: Fickle Finger of Fate
Twenty Years into the Future

Task: Work out how everyone interrelates before the fortune-teller reads everyone's future.

Twenty Years Later
You have won the Lotto and drive a great car, but have relationship difficulties.

Twenty Years Later
You have been having a passionate relationship with the best friend of the person who won the Lotto.

Twenty Years Later
You marry a wildly exciting but less than faithful partner who has a keen eye on the rest of your group!

Twenty Years Later
You become a fortune-teller and predict the rest of the group's futures.

Twenty Years Later
You gain a fortune and then gamble it away on the races and the casinos.

Worksheet: Fickle Finger of Fate
Thirty Years into the Future

Task: The television celebrity has his group of friends on his top rating show to interview them. What would the show be 'titled'? What questions might he ask?

Thirty Years Later
You are in jail and the rest of the group visit you.

Thirty Years Later
You have become a religious person and have given up your previous wild ways.

Thirty Years Later
Recently separated, you have hit the drink in a big way. No job, three kids and no money.

Thirty Years Later
You arrange a group reunion. How does it go?

Thirty Years Later
You have become a television celebrity with your own daytime TV show.

Worksheet: Fickle Finger of Fate—Forty Years Into the Future

Task
The Prime Minister offers two members of the group a job. Based on their lives to date, each member must make a case for what job they should be appointed to and why they should be chosen.

Forty Years Later
You have a deep-seated hatred for the person who was the TV celebrity in the past round.

Forty Years Later
You fall head over heels in love with the friend of the person who hit the drink in a big way.

Forty Years Later
You, you poor soul, arrange this reunion. How does it go?

Forty Years Later
You become Prime Minister and hold traditional values for the role of women and families.

Forty Years Later
You have become a family court lawyer and have a face-lift and a younger lover who is the child of the reunion organiser.

Worksheet: Fickle Finger of Fate
Fifty Years into The Future

Task

Each player looks back over their life. What would they change?

What were the hardest periods in their life? How did they get over them?

Fifty Years Later

Why are you supremely happy?

Now look back over your cards. What would you change? Why?

Fifty Years Later

Why are you depressed?

Now look back over your cards. What would you change? Why?

Fifty Years Later

Why are you angry and bitter?

Now look back over your cards. What would you change? Why?

Fifty Years Later

Why are you surrounded by a fantastic family?

Now look back over your cards. What would you change? Why?

Fifty Years Later

Why are you very rich and very fit and why do you play a lot of sport?

Now look back over your cards. What would you change? Why?

Session ten: Predictions

Purpose
To explore how well students might predict, even if they do not know.

Process
1. Hand out Estimations Quiz One to each student. Ask them to complete it on their own.
2. Form students into groups and repeat the task as a group.
3. Discuss questions.
4. Repeat process for Estimations Quiz Two.

Discussion questions
Is it difficult to guess?

How might you work out an answer when you have no idea of the correct figure?

After completing the second quiz, discuss whether students made better predictions in the first or second estimations quiz.

Answers for the Estimations Quiz 1
1. 1000
2. 244,820 sq km
3. 320 billion
4. 18,300
5. 4568
6. 50,612,000
7. 400 million
8. 392,819
9. 1,236,910,000
10. 1.5 million

Answers for Estimations Quiz 2
1. 19 kgs.
2. 100,000 hairs
3. 950 kms.
4. 206 bones
5. 350 bones
6. 25%
7. 1.8 litres.
8. 274 km per hour
9. 23,040 breaths
10. 415,000,000

ADOLESCENTS: SNAPPY IDEAS

Worksheet: Estimations Quiz One

Individually estimate a high and a low figure for each of the questions below. Then after you have done that try to come up with a group figure.

Question	Low	High	Group
1. The number of McDonalds Restaurants in Britain as at June 2004	....	....	....
2. The area in square kilometres of the United Kingdom	....	....	....
3. The number of Lego bricks sold over the past 50 years	....	....	....
4. The number of taxis in London	....	....	....
5. The number of taxis in metropolitan Birmingham	....	....	....
6. The number of international passengers that visit Heathrow airport, London, each year	....	....	....
7. The number of M & M chocolates produced world wide every day	....	....	....
8. The population of Manchester in January 2002	....	....	....
9. The population of China in January, 1999	....	....	....
10. The number of Barbie dolls sold every week	....	....	....

Worksheet: Estimations Quiz Two

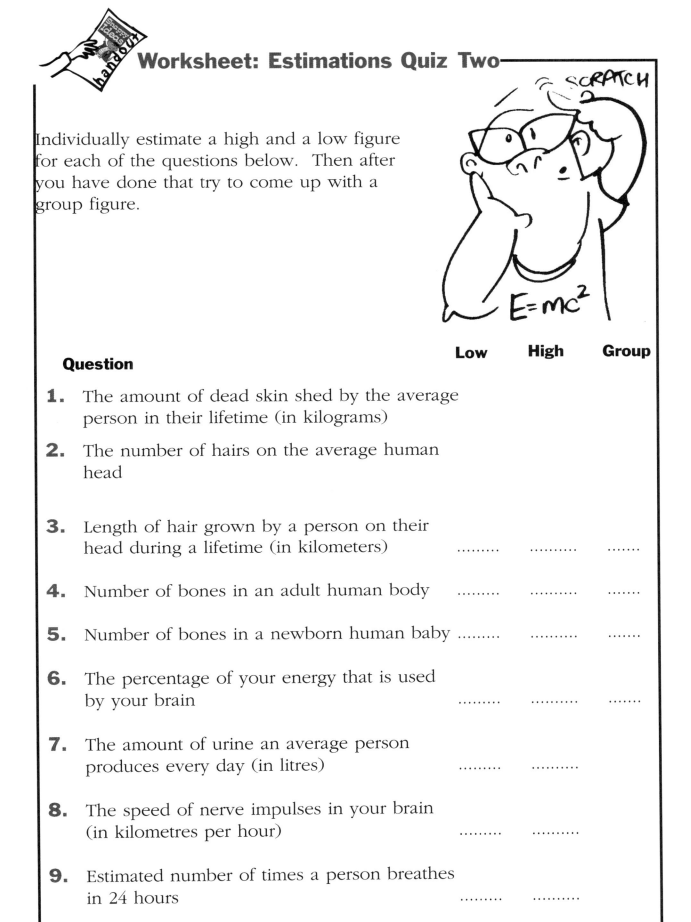

Individually estimate a high and a low figure for each of the questions below. Then after you have done that try to come up with a group figure.

Question	Low	High	Group
1. The amount of dead skin shed by the average person in their lifetime (in kilograms)			
2. The number of hairs on the average human head			
3. Length of hair grown by a person on their head during a lifetime (in kilometers)	....	....	....
4. Number of bones in an adult human body	....	....	....
5. Number of bones in a newborn human baby	....	....	....
6. The percentage of your energy that is used by your brain	....	....	....
7. The amount of urine an average person produces every day (in litres)	....	....	
8. The speed of nerve impulses in your brain (in kilometres per hour)	....	....	
9. Estimated number of times a person breathes in 24 hours	....	....	
10. Number of times people blink in a lifetime	....	....	....

ADOLESCENTS: SNAPPY IDEAS

Session eleven: Future Predictors

Purpose

To consider how the world might change.

Procedure

- Hand out worksheets.
- Ask students to complete.
- Collate the results of the future survey and discuss. Then create a discussion around the theme outlines below.

Discussion points

Can the future cause the present? (a forth-coming exam might cause you to study).

Can you see the past? (Consider seeing the light from stars that has taken so many light years to get here that you may be viewing a star that no longer exists).

Teacher notes: Become a Future Predictor

Predicting the future has a long history. Even the most admired predictors of the future sometimes gave puzzling advice and predictions. One of the most famous in all of history was the Oracle of Delphi in Greece.

According to the ancient Greeks, Delphi lay at the exact centre of the world. On the seventh day of each month the high Priestess, Pythia, would seat herself in the temple and, locked in an ecstatic trance, would wait for people to ask her questions.

Some examples were:

- King Croesus of Lydia wanted to know whether to go to war or to keep peace. The Oracle said, *"Go to war and destroy a great empire."* He went to war and his empire was destroyed.
- Lysander, the Spartan general, who had entered Athens in triumph was warned,

"I bid you guard against a roaring hoplite and a snake, cunning son of the earth, which attacks from behind the back." He was killed by a soldier with the emblem of a snake on his shield.

The Emperor Nero, fearing death, was told, *"Expect evil from 73."* Encouraged, he thought that he might live to be 73. In the event he was overthrown and forced to kill himself at the age of 31. Seventy-three turned out to be the age of his successor, Galba.

*Information from: Davies N, (1997) Europe : A History, Pimlico Press, London

Consider and discuss the following trends:

Jeremy Rivkin in the US claims that 90 million out of 124 million jobs are vulnerable to being replaced by machines, since the 1950s blue-collar jobs have dropped from 33% of all jobs to less than 12%.

In America people are spending more on home entertainment systems, text messaging, televisions in cars and down-loadable music than on kitchens.

Worksheet: Future Survey Form

This is a survey about future trends. There are no right or wrong answers.

There can't be - the future hasn't happened yet.

1. What do you think will be the three most important changes in the world in the next five to ten years?

   a. ....
   ....

   b. ....
   ....

   c. ....
   ....

2. What are three things that will become less important over the next five to ten years?

   a. ....
   ....

   b. ....
   ....

   c. ....
   ....

Session twelve: Predictions about Me

Purpose

For students to examine predictions about themselves.

Process

1. Ask students if they might be able to predict anything about their own lives:
   - tomorrow
   - in one year's time
   - in ten years' time?
2. Complete the worksheet.
3. Share answers with the class.

Discussion questions

What are the most important influences on your future?

Why do some people seemingly change course in life? (For example, catastrophic event, drugs, discovery, sudden insight?)

Worksheet: Predictions about Me

Briefly describe where you expect to be in ten years' time under each of these headings.

Family

....
....
....

Career

....
....
....

Wealth

....
....
....

Interests/hobbies

....
....
....

Friends

....
....
....

Health

....
....
....

Level of contentment…Very Unhappy   1 2 3 4 5 6 7 8 9 10   Very Happy

Session thirteen: Fashion parade

Purpose
To explore ways of understanding others.

Preparation
Collect a number of pictures, objects, pieces of artwork, music, clothing, cosmetics, sports equipment etc. (Alternatively, students could be asked to bring items.)

Newspapers, tape, scissors, felt pens.

Procedure
1. Place items around the room.
2. Ask students to take a seat in the circle.
3. Brainstorm a list of well-known people who are familiar to all of the students.
4. Choosing one well-known person at a time, ask students in pairs to think of one word that most indicates who that person is. For instance, words for a famous footballer might be courageous, skilfull or sportsperson, while words for a pop star might be singer, musical or creative.
5. Proceed around the circle for each person writing down the words under each well-known person's name.

6. Discuss whether the words varied more for some well-known people than others.
7. Ask the students to stand and walk around the room looking at the items that have been placed. Ask the students to choose an item that represents them in some way and then return to the circle with the item and take a seat.
8. Go around the circle asking the students to explain how the item represents them.
9. Ask students to form into groups and hand out newspaper and materials.
10. Inform students that they are fashion designers. Their task is to create an outfit from newspaper in 10 to 15 minutes! There will be a fashion parade at the end using one of the team members as the model.

 (NB: If teachers prefer, they might allocate different types of outfits to different teams, for example, a suit, a jockey's outfit, a dress, a hat and bag etc.)

11. Conduct fashion parade.
12. Thank all of the students for their efforts and commend their creativity!
13. Discuss questions.

Discussion questions

How much do you learn about people based on clothing?

What other ways help you to know about a person?

Session fourteen: Great First Lines of Books

Purpose
To explore what makes a book or person interesting.

Preparation
Photocopy worksheets.

Process
1. Ask students to sit in a circle.
2. Go around the circle asking students to complete the sentence:
   - One of my favourite books is…
3. Discuss:
   - What books students enjoy reading
   - How students choose a book to read.
4. Hand out ' Great First Lines of Books' worksheet.
5. Ask students to complete the worksheet.
6. When they have completed the worksheet, proceed around the circle asking students to nominate the books that received their highest and lowest ratings.
7. Discuss questions.

Discussion questions
What are the ingredients of a really good first line in a book?

What are the ingredients of a really good book?

Brainstorm the similarities between an interesting book and an interesting person.

# Worksheet: Great First Lines of Books

Rate the following first lines from books.

10 = very likely to read on

0 = wouldn't be bothered reading on.

Worksheet: Great First Lines of Books

"The first time I laid eyes on Terry Lennox he was drunk in a Rolls Royce Silver Wraith outside the terrace of The Dancers."
Raymond Chandler, The Long Good Bye

"Whenever my mother talks to me, she begins the conversation as if we were already in the middle of an argument."
Amy Tan, The Kitchen God's Wife

"Every nine and half years I see Amanda."
Elliot Perlman, Three Dollars

"Whether I shall turn out to be the hero of my own life, or whether that station will be held by anybody else, these pages must show."
Charles Dickens, David Copperfield

"The hospital again, and the echo of my reluctant feet through the long, empty corridors."
Sally Morgan, My Place

"The two cops were virtually invisible."
Shane Maloney, The Brush Off

"I can hardly bear to write about it"
Paul Jennings, Singenpoo strikes again

Worksheet: Great First Lines of Books

Now write one opening line of a story, one that would really make you read on.

Session fifteen: The Day I Discovered My Bottom

Purpose
To explore how people make judgments about others.

Preparation
Photocopy worksheets.

Process
1. Ask students to sit in a circle.
2. Distribute The Day I Discovered My Bottom and worksheet.
3. Ask students to read The Day I Discovered My Bottom and complete the worksheet.
4. Proceed around the circle, asking students:
   - Which essay they rated most highly?
   - Which factors most influenced their judgments?
5. Ask students to stand up. Inform them you are going to read some statements. If they agree they should proceed to one end of the room, if they disagree they should proceed to the opposite end of the room. If they are unsure, they may choose to stand in the middle of the room.
   - Most people have been bullied at some time.
   - Most people have bullied someone at some time.
   - Boys bully more than girls.
   - Boys like to hang out in groups more than girls.
   - Girls talk about feelings more than boys.
   - Love is blind.
   - Most people love their pets.
   - Most people can love someone of the same gender.
6. Discuss questions.

Discussion questions
Brainstorm the things people are making judgments about all the time for example, clothing, make-up, television shows, news items and other people.

How often do you make wrong judgments?

What are the most difficult judgments to make?

Worksheet: The Day I Discovered My Bottom

Essay one: The Day I discovered my Bottom

Now, bottoms aren't easy things to discover generally. They sneak around behind you out of sight. They only make themselfs known at the most unmentionable moments and rarely say a good word for themselves. The first discoverer of the bottom was the daring, dashing adventuruss Connie Tortionist who was so flexible she was able to turn herself inside out. It was only after years of flexibility training, the I finally travelled around myself to discover my bottom for the first time.

Mark . . . . . .

Essay two: The Day I discovered my bottom

My bottom and I have had a life long friendship - it supports me when I need a rest and I put my weight on it. I rely on it, depend on it even. I turned around one day and it was their. I didn't discover my bottom – it found me!

Mark . . . . . .

Essay three: The Day I discovered my bottom

A bottom is a tricky thing to lose. I mean it can't fall off can it ? Lot's of people complan bout theres saying theyd like a smaller won or a different shape but most people shood shut up about it. There is more important things than bottoms in the world to discover.

Mark . . . . . .

ADOLESCENTS: SNAPPY IDEAS

Worksheet: The Day I Discovered My Bottom

Instructions

Give a mark out of ten for each essay.

Write down the factors that influenced your judgment.

Essay one /10	**Essay two .... /10**	**Essay three ...... /10 .**
....	....	....
....	....	....
....	....	....
....	....	....
....	....	....
....	....	....
....	....	....

What marks would you give if you were told to make judgments based on:

- **a.** Humour
- **b.** Grammar and spelling
- **c.** Logical thinking

Describe a time when you had a strong opinion and later changed your mind ....
....
....

How do you make judgements about other people? ....
....
....

How do people make judgements about you? ....
....
....

Session sixteen: What's Cool?

Purpose
To increase students' awareness of the influences to conform.

Preparation
Photocopy sufficient handouts (on next page) for each student.

Process
1. Ask students to sit in a circle and to follow the instructions you are about to give. (Students might like to record their answers.)
2. Give the following instructions:
   - Select a number between 2 and 9. Keep this number to yourself.
   - Multiply your number by nine.
   - If this number has 2 digits add them together, so you get one number.
   - Now subtract 5 from this number.
   - Relate this number to the alphabet so that 1 is the letter A, 2 is the letter B, 3 is the letter C and so on.
   - Think of a country that begins with that letter.
   - Take the second letter of that country's name and think of an animal that begins with that letter.
3. Ask: How many people are thinking of an elephant in Denmark?
4. Ask whether students believe they were unknowingly led to their answer, or whether they realised where they were being led?
5. Hand out worksheets and ask students to complete.
6. Ask students to compare their answers with the person next to them, and to see how many were the same.
7. Brainstorm a list of 'What's cool?'
8. Discuss questions.
9. Proceed around the circle asking students to complete the sentence:
   - The coolest thing in the world is…

Discussion questions
Explain whether 'coolness' influences what people buy?
Explain whether advertising tries to manipulate people?

Worksheet: What's Cool?

Answer the following questions.
Name three singers, bands or types of music that you consider to be cool.

1. ....
2. ....
3. ....

Name three singers, bands or types of music you consider to be uncool.

1. ....
2. ....
3. ....

Circle the following that you consider to be cool:

Rap music	Lace	Jennifer Lopez	McDonalds
Paris Hilton	Tartan	Leather jackets	Britney Spears
Politicians	Reality TV	McDonalds	FHM (magazine)
Drugs	Horse riding	Coca Cola	Short skirts
The Beatles	Having a dog	Action movies	Success

What does 'cool' mean?

....
....
....

How does 'coolness' influence people's judgements?

....
....
....

ADOLESCENTS: SNAPPY IDEAS

Session seventeen: Nothin', Dunno and Whatever!

Purpose

To increase students' awareness of the messages they get to conform.

Preparation

Video of advertisements, magazines, direct mail items etc.

Pieces of large paper, coloured pens for drawing.

Process

1. Ask students to sit in a circle.
2. Show advertisements and discuss with students:
   - What is the aim of each advertisement?
   - Which techniques are being used to influence people?
   - How effective is each advertisement?
3. Divide students into groups of three or four. Tell them they have 15 minutes to come up with an advertising campaign and that they will need to present their campaign to the rest of the class. They can create a billboard, a poster, a jingle – whatever they want. The aim of the activity is to sell the idea to the rest of the class. Then assign the following campaign to different groups:
   - The aim of your group is to get as many students as possible to sign up for a school subject called, 'Nothin'.
   - The aim of your group is to get as many people as possible to buy a breakfast cereal called 'Dunno'.
   - The aim of your group is to get as many people as possible to buy a new drink called 'Whatever'.
   - The aim of your group is to get as many people as possible to attend a decision-making programme for the undecided called, 'Make Up Your Mind.'
   - The aim of your group is to convince people to become teachers called, 'It's not as bad as it looks!'
   - The aim of your group is to get as many young people as possible to sign up for a programme on, 'How to Deal with Difficult Adults.'
4. Each group then presents their campaign.
5. After each presentation, ask the group to rate from 1 - 10 whether the advertising was convincing.
6. Discuss questions.
7. Proceed around the circle and ask students to complete the sentence:
   - The best advertisement I have ever seen is…

Discussion questions

What is the best advertisement on television?
Why is it the best advertisement?

Session eighteen: Popular Culture

Purpose
To increase students' awareness of the messages they get to conform.

Preparation
Video of a soap for example Neighbours or EastEnders.

One copy of worksheet on the next page for each student.

 (NB: If a teacher is unable to tape a show, popular teenage magazines could be used, or teachers could ask students to complete the worksheet from memory.)

Procedure
1. Show the video or magazine pictures.
2. Ask students to describe what they know about the characters.
3. Complete the worksheets.
4. Discuss answers to the worksheets.
5. Brainstorm a list of words that most accurately describe the range of characters represented in the video (or popular magazine).
6. Make another column, and brainstorm a list of words that most accurately describe the range of characters in the local community.
7. Using the lists, break students into groups and handout large poster sized sheets of paper and drawing materials. Some groups draw and label the typical popular culture character, and the other groups draw and label the typical local character.
8. Discuss questions.

Discussion questions
What message does popular culture give about 'normal' people?

How does popular culture differ from your experiences in everyday life?

In what ways are you influenced by popular culture characters?

Worksheet: Popular Culture

After watching the video (or reading the magazine) answer these questions.

What was the most common age of the characters?

....
....

How many characters had disabilities?

....
....

What types of family groups were most commonly represented? (Nuclear family, single parent, extended family, same gender couples etc)

....
....

What sorts of relationships were most common? (friendship, sexual etc)

....
....

What types of body shapes were most common for males?

....
....

Females?

....
....

What is the most common ethnic group represented?

....
....

Session nineteen: The Winners!

Purpose
To explore the factors that indicate success.

Process
1. Break students into groups.
2. Distribute board games and dice.
3. Demonstrate to students how to build their profiles of a person.
4. Ask students to answer questions in a group.
5. Each group appoints a person to report back to the larger group.
6. Discuss questions.

Discussion questions
What is the opposite of success?

How is success portrayed in popular culture?

Do indicators of success change with age?

Do indicators of success vary between people?

Explain whether it is important to be successful.

At what is it important for you to be most successful?

Worksheet: The Winners!

Roll your dice once for each row and circle the corresponding box. Answer the questions.

	1	2	3	4	5	6
Friends	A variety of friends of different ages	No really close friendships	One friend who recently moved away	Moves from one group to another	Some friends are into drugs and petty crime	Has hung out with the same group for years
Family	Regularly visits only surviving grandparent	Lives with mother. Refuses to speak to father	Spends a lot of time with large extended family	Grieving twin brother becoming paraplegic	Only child who never seems to please parents	Expecting a new BMW for birthday
School	Excels at sport	Top of the class in most subjects	Works hard, but struggles in most subjects	Participates in most things	Always seems to be in trouble	Often truants
Achievement	Winner of a beauty contest	Computer game expert	An acrobat on a skateboard	Watches the most hours of television in the class	Has a high paying part-time job	Surfing champion
Romance	Very popular	Has a steady relationship	Always seems to go for the wrong person	Gets teased about being gay	Never seems to get beyond a one-night stand	Self-conscious, shows little interest
Attitude	Arrogant	Competitive	Confident	Modest	Positive	Negative

Worksheet: The Winners!

"LIFE LOTTO"

Write down the profile of your person.
....
....
....
....

Try to describe your person, explaining what they are like.
....
....
....
....

List the factors in each column.

Indicators of success	Indicators of failure nor failure	Indicators of neither success

How would you rate the above person on a scale of one to ten?

Unsuccessful **1 2 3 4 5** Average **6 7 8 9 10** Very successful

Would your rating change if you learned that your person was:
- 15 years old?
- 30 years old?
- 50 years old?

Session twenty: Dating Agency

Purpose
For students to think about different types of relationships.

Process
1. Read out Dating Agency advertisements.
2. Ask students to guess the age and gender of the person in each advertisement.
3. Ask students to give reasons for their guess.
4. Ask students, if they had to date one person, explain whom they would most likely choose.
5. Distribute the Relationship cards, one to each student, and ask them one at a time to place the cards along a continuum, rating them from 'Most Important' to 'Least Important', in response to the question, 'What is the most important characteristic you look for in a friend?' As each student places their card ask them to explain their placement. When they are placing their card, students may move other cards, as long as they give an explanation for the change.
6. When completed, ask what students would change if the question had been, 'What is the most important characteristic you look for in a romantic relationship?'
7. Discuss questions.

Discussion questions
What are the different types of relationships students have? E.g., friends, parents, lovers, colleagues etc.

How do these characteristics change with age?

Which characteristics are always important?

Worksheet: Dating Agency

Lonely Hearts

Young, good looking, tall and swarthy, just come down from country, looking to share a good time, enjoys barbecues, larking about and rodeos.

Romantic type, sensitive and traditional, enjoys most things, especially reading, walking, candlelit dinners and good conversation.

Outdoor type. Loves sports, 'physical' activity, drinking and movies. Seeks like-minded fun loving gal. Pref. blonde.

Biker who lives for the open road. Looking for a pillion. Want to join me?

Do you hate the government? I'm a rap dancin', skateboardin', cool dude, got rhythm and attitude. Check me out!

Attractive, well-heeled, shy and thoughtful. Secret desires that would like to share. Seeking handsome 20-30 year old professional guy.

Nurse who loves caring for people. Energetic, great cook, loud, giggly and friendly. Never a dull moment. Will meet your every need.

Lonely new arrival. Traditional values. Hard working. Reliable. Seeks sincere relationship.

Dreaming of a life with a mate, 2 children, 2 cars, a house with a garden and swimming pool, annual holidays by the sea. If you share my dream, you are the one for me.

I'm loyal, pretty and friendly. I love babies, and I want someone to make them with. Do you love babies too?

Explain whether it is possible to know what

Explain whether it is possible to know what people are like from these advertisements?

....
....

How do young people usually get to know each other?

....
....
....

Write a description of yourself for a dating agency.

....
....

Worksheet: Relationship Cards

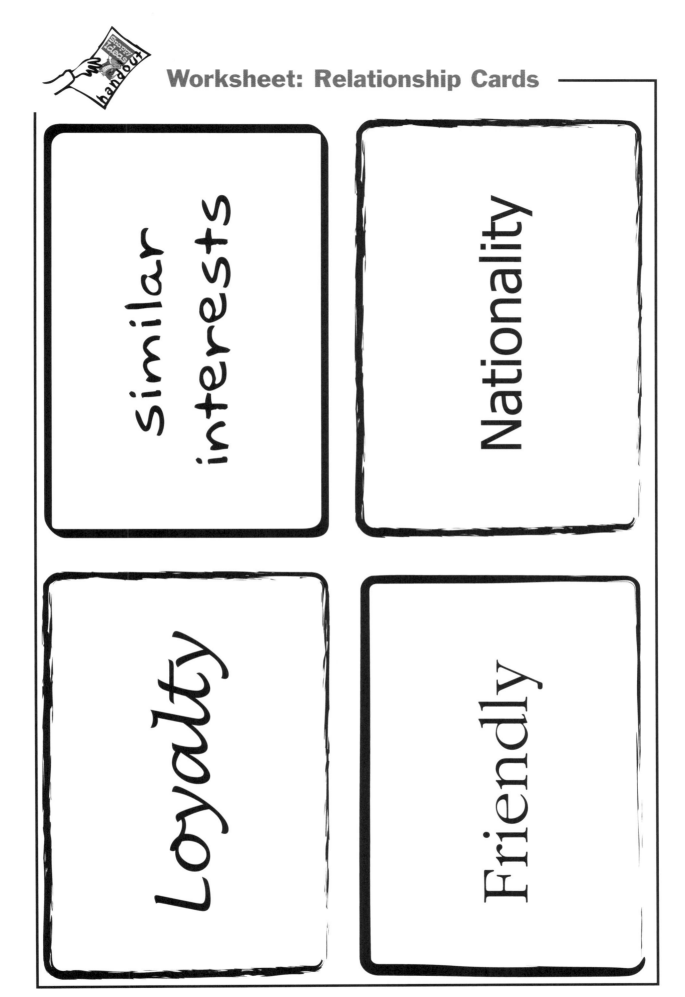

ADOLESCENTS: SNAPPY IDEAS

Worksheet: Relationship Cards

- Trustworthiness
- Good Looks
- Trendiness
- Gender

ADOLESCENTS: SNAPPY IDEAS

Worksheet: Relationship Cards

- Good manners
- Sense of humour
- Hygiene
- Sexual orientation

Worksheet: Relationship Cards

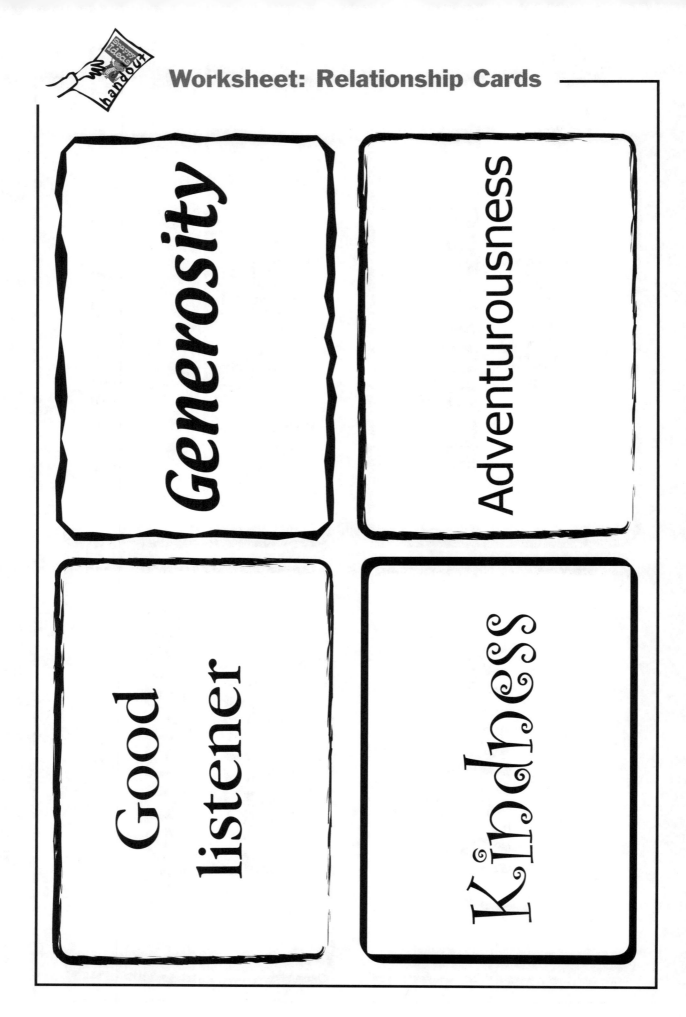

Worksheet: Relationship Cards

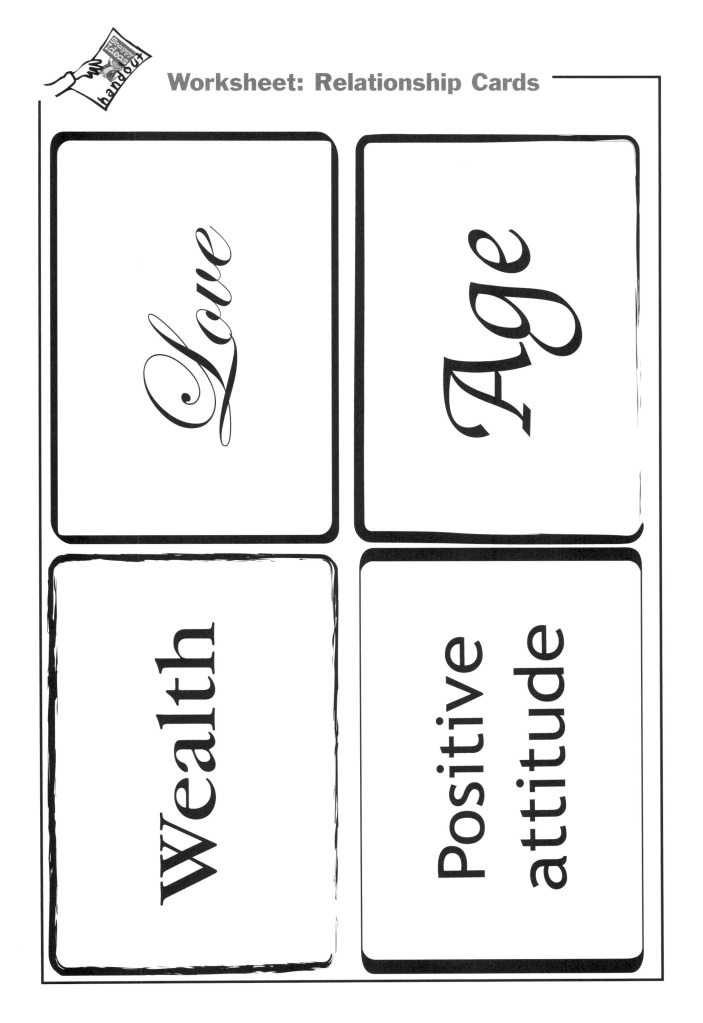

ADOLESCENTS: SNAPPY IDEAS

Session twenty-one: Careers – what am I good at?

Purpose

To think about matching skills with careers.

Explanatory note: The following activity is based on Gardiner's original six intelligences to encourage students to think about how their skills might influence their choice of career. These intelligences are linguistic, mathematic, spatial, musical, kinaesthetic and emotional. Other categories have been avoided for the sake of simplicity.

Process

1. Hand out a skill card to each student.
2. Put a 'Very useful' sign at one end of the room and a 'Not useful' sign at the other end of the room.
3. Read out different learning situations.
4. Ask students to rate how useful their skill is to each situation by standing with their card along the continuum. The closer they are to either end, the more strongly they agree with the signs.
5. At the end of the activity, consider the discussion questions as a class.
6. Ask students to complete the self-test.
7. Ask students to explain the skill category in which they consider themselves to be most proficient.
8. Brainstorm the types of jobs that suit each skill category.

Discussion questions

Explain whether most people choose a career based on what they are good at, or what they enjoy.

Learning situations *(NB: Use all, choose only a few or make up your own situations.)*

Building a bridge.

Promoting a new brand of chocolate.

Writing a piece of music.

Designing new clothes.

Listening to people talk about themselves.

Making a movie.

Fixing a tractor.

Growing vegetables.

Looking after someone who is unwell.

Diagnosing an illness.

Lending money.

Arresting a criminal.

Fighting for a cause.

Worksheet: Skill cards

Body

I am good at practical pursuits. I am a dancer, a gymnast, an athlete, a model, a rapper, a tight-rope walker, a sporting enthusiast, a stunt person, a farmer, a carpenter.

Music

I am good at music. I conduct orchestras, I play musical instruments, I set music to movies, I play in a band, I write songs, I sing and I write advertising ditties.

Worksheet: Skill cards

Visual

I am good visually. I build houses and buildings. I am a fashion designer, a painter, a sculptor, an interior decorator, an animation artist, a museum curator, a truck driver.

People

I am emotionally intelligent. I understand feelings. I am self-aware. I am a psychologist, a social worker, a nurse, a healer, a spiritual person, a manager of people.

Worksheet: Skill cards

Word

I am good with words. I am a writer, a politician, a poet, an advertising consultant, a real estate agent, a journalist, an editor, a conversationalist, a storyteller, a script writer, a comedian.

Logic

I am good with mathematics and logic. I am an accountant, a scientist, a business manager, a bookkeeper, a bank teller, an engineer, a pharmacist, a stock broker, a computer programmer

Not Useful

Worksheet: Self test – What are my strengths?

Answer these questions either 'yes' or 'no' to get an indication of your skills. These are not conclusive tests. They are just a guide to help you to think about the different professions that might suit you.

Word/linguistic

	Yes	No
I enjoy reading.	☐	☐
I remember by writing down my thoughts.	☐	☐
I get a feeling of satisfaction from using words well.	☐	☐
Other students ask me when they don't know the meaning of a word.	☐	☐
I am confident about doing well in English classes.	☐	☐

Mathematics/logic

	Yes	No
I enjoy facts and figures.	☐	☐
I remember things by putting them into patterns or sequences.	☐	☐
People sometimes compliment me on my memory of sporting (or other) statistics.	☐	☐
I can tell when people are making things up by their contradictions and inconsistencies.	☐	☐
I am confident and do well in mathematics classes.	☐	☐

Spatial

	Yes	No
I enjoy drawing or designing things.	☐	☐
I remember things by associating them with objects.	☐	☐
I look at the pictures in a book or manual before reading the words.	☐	☐
I can imagine what objects look like from every angle (sideways, above or below).	☐	☐
I am confident and do well in art and graphics classes.	☐	☐

Worksheet: Self test – what are my strengths?
Continued...

Body/doing | Yes | No

I enjoy dancing and/or playing sport.

I remember how to do things by using them.

I like being outdoors and/or making things.

Other people sometimes say to me things like, 'Can't you keep still?'

I feel confident in physical education and/or practical subjects.

Music | Yes | No

I enjoy music.

I associate music with memories.

I can communicate my feelings through music.

I often have tunes in my head.

I play a musical instrument.

People/emotional | Yes | No

I enjoy talking about myself and other people.

I tend to associate my feelings with memories.

I am sensitive to the feelings of other people.

I manage my feelings so they have a positive effect on my actions.

I feel confident when speaking to others about their feelings.

Session twenty-two: What's My Career?

Purpose
To examine different industries.

Process
- Ask students to select an industry to study.
- Each student investigates an industry and reports on that industry to the class.
- Students complete worksheets, rating each industry out of 10 in terms of a series of criteria: Interest, Money, Scope and Skill match.

Discussion questions
What are the most important influences on career choice?
Why might it be sensible to aim for an industry, rather than a specific career?
What industry did you rate most highly? Why?

Worksheet: What's My Career?

Rate each of the following industry categories out of ten with ten equalling 'a lot' and zero equalling 'very little.'

Explanation

Interest: Is this industry interesting to you?
Money: Are jobs generally well paid in this industry?
Scope: Is there a wide variety of jobs in this industry?
Skill match: Do the skills required in this industry match your personal skills?

Industry	Interest	Money	Scope	Skill match	Total
Human resources	....	....	....	....	....
Media/advertising	....	....	....	....	....
Education	....	....	....	....	....
Building/construction	....	....	....	....	....
Manufacturing	....	....	....	....	....
Transport	....	....	....	....	....
Health	....	....	....	....	....
Agriculture	....	....	....	....	....
Beauty/fashion	....	....	....	....	....
Law/politics	....	....	....	....	....
Environment	....	....	....	....	....
Sport/recreation	....	....	....	....	....
Information technology	....	....	....	....	....
Finance	....	....	....	....	....
Other	....	....	....	....	....

Bibliography

Fuller, A. (2003) *Help Your Child Succeed at School*, Queenscliff: Inyahead Press.

Fuller, A (2001) A blueprint for building social competencies in children and adolescents, *Australian Journal of Middle Schooling*, 1,1,40-48.

Fuller, A., McGraw, K and Goodyear, M (2002) *Bungy-Jumping Through Life: a developmental framework for the promotion of resilience*, In L. Rowling, G. Martin and L. Walker, (eds.) Mental Health and Young People Sydney: McGraw/Hill.

Miller,D.C. and Byrnes, J.P. (2001) To achieve or not to achieve: a self-regulation perspective on adolescents/academic decision-making, *Journal of Educational Psychology*, 93,4,677-685

Perkins,D. (1995) *Outsmarting IQ- the emerging science of learnable intelligence*, New York: Free Press

Root-Bernstein,R and Root-Bernstein,M (1999) *Sparks of Genius - the thirteen thinking tools of the world's most creative people*, Mariner: Boston.

Sternberg, R.J. (2001) Why schools should teach for wisdom: the balance theory of wisdom in educational settings?, *Educational Psychologist*, 36,4,227-245.

Don't forget to visit our website for all our latest publications, news and reviews.

www.luckyduck.co.uk

New publications every year on our specialist topics:

- **Emotional Literacy**
- **Self-esteem**
- **Bullying**
- **Positive Behaviour Management**
- **Circle Time**
- **Anger Management**
- **Asperger's Syndrome**
- **Eating Disorders**

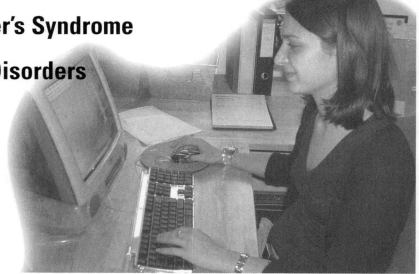